10 STRATEGIES FOR DEVELOPING RESILIENT AND CONFIDENT CHILDREN

TERRY ROSS, PH.D.

ISBN: 978-1-7367989-0-4

Dedication

This book is dedicated to all the parents, teachers and mentors that work hard every day to develop resilient and confident children.

This book is also dedicated to my wife and daughter. Thanks for loving and believing in me.

Table of Contents

INTRODUCTION

Ten Strategies for Developing Resilient and Confident Children is my contribution to a larger conversation about developing resilient, happy, and confident children. Parenting, teaching, and mentoring are challenging undertakings, but immensely rewarding and enjoyable, especially when we have the desired outcomes. We are constantly bombarded with information and research on what it takes to raise children. Most of us can agree that we want our children to be healthy and confident, we also want them to be reasonably happy. I added happy last because happiness is a state of mind most often found in one's confidence. The happiest people that I have been around always seems to be content with themselves and are always planning or working on something.

Morgan Stanley (2016), in a report on the cost of raising children stated that it cost $245,000 to raise a child from birth to age 18. My parents raised 9 of us and may not have made this much money in 5 years. My parents also did not have access to the information we have today to help us raise healthy, resilient and confident children. I am raising my daughter with most of what I learned from my parents because we can never go wrong with raising our children to understand integrity, hard work, resilience, perseverance, tenacity, grit and compassion. Those are the lessons that my parents gave me, and it did not cost nearly $245,000 for them to raise my siblings and me. Sometimes we need to take a step back and make sure that we ground our children with some essential foundational characteristics. It does not cost money to gift our children with values and virtues. We cannot always outsource the skills, values and virtues that our children need modeled consistently. Parenting is heart work and hard work. We must put our heart into it, and it will take some hard work on our behalf.

When we know better, we do better. This book outlines some strategies that I have learned as an educator, coach, leader, and father that have been added to my toolbox to help strengthen my capacity to help develop children's confidence. I like to focus on confidence because it is most associated with having the ability and courage to endeavor into new tasks, hobbies, careers and mindsets. Confidence also arms you with the mindset to hold tight to our dreams and complete a task.

We spend so much time wanting our children to have high self-esteem, that we often overlook the role that confidence plays in having healthy self-esteem. Self-esteem is often associated with feeling good about yourself. You can feel good because you have some new clothes or a new car or maybe even a fresh haircut. Self-confidence is associated with believing in your abilities to accomplish goals. When we assist our children with setting goals and achieving them, that is one way we help them develop confidence. We also develop confidence by ensuring they read regularly, making sure that they complete their homework as well as ensuring that they study consistently. I choose SELF-CONFIDENCE because when we are confident, having healthy self-esteem is usually within reach!!!

It is easier to build strong children than to repair broken men.

Frederick Douglass (1817-1895)

SELF-ESTEEM
VS
SELF-CONFIDENCE

I CHOOSE

SELF-CONFIDENCE

HELP YOUR CHILD BUILD SELF-CONFIDENCE

I can
Do It

Strategy One

I Believe In You

THE FOUR MOST

IMPORTANT WORDS YOU CAN

SAY TO A CHILD IS:

I

BELIEVE

IN

YOU

Let your children know that you BELIEVE IN THEM. We need to tell our children that we believe in them and tell them often. Yes, we show our children that we believe in them; however, we need to say it, our words have power. We need to tell our loved ones that we believe in them. We all feel stronger and more confident when we know that someone is in our corner. One of the most major concerns that children have is "Do I matter." Children want to know that someone is there for them. They do not care about all the other things if they see that they have someone in their corner. They will have the confidence to try new things and develop new skills because they have someone there to encourage them and to believe in them when things are not going well.

We must believe in our children when they are conducting themselves in a way that is not consistent with what they want to accomplish in life. If they are going to be in the band, are they practicing their instrument at home, or do they just show up to band practice? One of the hardest things for parents to do is to allow children to be themselves. Yes, we do have to give our children space to explore and find their interests. It is also essential that we provide guidance because of the amount of information that is available to young people. Make sure that we take time and look our children in the eye and say "I Believe in you."

It is necessary to stop and take time to look at them when we are saying "I Believe You". It is important that our children know that we are serious and that we are there for them. This will help our children persevere when they face challenges because they know that they represent more than themselves, because you believe in them.

Strategy Two

Invest In Your Children

OUR CHILDREN ARE OUR NOW!!!

WHAT WE INVEST INTO THEM WILL BE OUR FUTURE!!!

LET'S SPEAK LIFE INTO OUR CHILDREN AND GIVE THEM THE SKILLS THAT THEY NEED TO LIVE LIFE MORE ABUNDANTLY!!

We must raise children for their time and not for our time. Therefore, we must allow our children to be a part of something bigger than them, like a club, organization or a sport. It is those experiences that will put them around their peers and teach them life lessons. Companies and organizations are looking for people that are collaborators, problem solvers and team players. It is difficult for our children to acquire any of those skills if we do not provide them with the opportunities to learn from and interact with other people. It is ok for our children to play some video games and spend some time on the screen, but that cannot be the only thing that they do. Encourage them to get out and be a part of something at school, in the community or at their local place of worship. It is vital that we invest into our children so that they can develop the skills that are necessary to have a bright, vibrant and healthy future that is filled with abundance.

We do not know the jobs that our children will have to be prepared for in the future. The jobs that the preschoolers will have, have yet to be invented. That is why it is important for us to allow our children to be a part of the 'now' so that they can have experiences that will help them shape the future and not just respond to the future.

Strategy Three

Preparation: Work Today

WORK

TODAY

FOR A BETTER

TOMORROW...

Teach children that you must work today for a better tomorrow. If you listen to children, you always hear them say, when they try to comfort a friend or family member, “it’s ok, you’ll do better next time.” We have all seen videos online where an adult is in a crisis, and you will see a toddler saying, “it’s ok, I’m here with you.” Our children are born to look for a better tomorrow. Negativity and hate are taught. Whether it is intentional or through observation, negativity and hate are taught.

We must teach and model optimism as well as, self-efficacy for our children. Optimism is also the ability to put in the work for a better tomorrow. In other words, we must teach our children that if you want a better tomorrow, you must work for it today. Nothing comes easy, and nothing is free. Even free is not free. We teach optimism by staying positive and not giving up. Our children must see us persevere in the face of challenges. It is ok for our children to know when there are some challenges. It is healthy for them to see us work through challenging situations. That is how children learn optimism and perseverance. We work for a better tomorrow.

Children must know that if they want to be a better reader, they must practice reading to be better tomorrow. It is the same thing if they are going to be a better cross-country runner, they are going to have to practice to get better. Optimism does not mean that we are smiling all the time and lead our children to believe that life is always fun and happy. It means that we teach them to trouble shoot situations and work through obstacles and not let problems and obstacles stop them from achieving their goals.

STRATEGY FOUR

A Love for Learning: Read Daily

HELP YOUR CHILDREN DEVELOP A LOVE FOR LEARNING.

HELP THEM BE STRONG AVID READERS!!!

THE MORE YOU KNOW, THE MORE YOU GROW!!!

Children must learn how to read and they must also develop a love for reading. A passion for reading leads to a love for information. Information is the key to development and especially self-development. I have heard so many successful people talk about how much they read. They are continually developing themselves, to keep up with the times and to get ahead of the times. They help set the trend, or least benefit for having been on the ground floor or cutting edge of the next big thing.

Knowledge is Power! The use of knowledge is even more powerful. It is a game changer! Being able to read is essential. I do not care how many YouTube videos you can watch to learn how to do something. You still need to know how to read. Please set a schedule for your children to read for at least 30 minutes daily. The more you know, the more you grow. KNOWLEDGE IS POWER!!!

Curiosity is necessary for proper human growth and development. Our children need to be trained to read daily. In this age of information and digital access, our children need to be able to read and read critically, with understanding. We cannot depend on the news to gives us all the information that we need. Therefore, if we want our children to be on the cutting edge and informed, they need to learn to read and read well with an understanding. If your child struggles with reading, do not try to hide it or make excuses for them. Lean in and become an advocate. If your child continues to struggle, it could be dyslexia or some other concern that they can get the proper support to help them become strong readers. If you are not a strong reader as an adult, now is the time to become stronger. You can learn with your child.

I know that it is difficult to entertain all the questions that our children ask; however, we must encourage them to ask questions. Our default setting is to say, “stop asking so many questions.” Again, in this digital era we do not have to answer all of the questions. We can guide them to the answer with a search engine. Let your children ask all the questions they want to ask, also teach them how to find the answer to those questions, now you have a little researcher on your hand. At this point, you can ask them questions and send them to find the answer for you.

It is healthy to encourage curiosity, ask them questions and spend time helping them to learn to love reading. The best way is to model the love of reading.

Strategy Five

Teach Perseverance: Do not Quit

Teach your children positive affirmations (Positive Self-Talk) because sometimes we must encourage ourselves. We might as well start them to learn to affirm themselves at a young age. This will help build resilience, so that they will know that we will meet challenges and obstacles, but that is no reason to quit.

Our children need to know that negative situations and negative people in the world will discourage them and lead them to doubt themselves. When we teach our children positive affirmations, we give them the tools they need to resist the temptation of mediocrity and a habit of self-sabotage as well as failure.

We should never let our children say what they cannot do. We should never let our children hear us say what we cannot do. When we allow our children to say, "I cannot do this or that," we will enable them to put limits on their life. We will allow them to stop growing. As adults, we should never say what we cannot do. Maybe we do not like doing certain things or we are unwilling to learn how to do it, but we all can do whatever we are willing to put in the work and effort to do. It is all about effort and not luck. I have had people to tell me that I am lucky, NO, I work hard, and I GRIND!!! I BELIEVE IN ME!!! Never let what anyone else thinks of you put limits on your life, we need to teach our children that it is all about what we believe. I BELIEVE THE BEST IS

YET TO BE!!! Let us keep believing and keep working hard because we are not there YET!!! Below are some affirmations that we can teach our children:

I am worthy! I am a winner! I will do my best every time! I work hard! I am special! I am loved! My family loves me!

STRATEGY SIX

Communicate: Listen To Your Children

LISTEN TO YOUR CHILDREN...

WE ALL WANT TO BE HEARD.

WHEN WE LISTEN TO CHILDREN WE ARE ACTUALLY TEACHING THEM TO COMMUNICATE .

I used to have a neighbor that would say, "The sweetest thing in the world is an understanding." The best way to teach our children to be great communicators is to listen to them and help them make sense of the world. As adults, once someone listens to us and allows us to explain why we feel, the way we feel, it helps us to arrive at closure, a better understanding and most of all, we feel like we mattered. Children need to feel the same way, they are young people in training to become adults. We should give children every opportunity to practice and know what it is like to listen and to be listened to.

Listening is a huge part of communication. We have too many young people dependent on technology and twitter style communication and to converse at any real length with them is sometimes painful. We all need to take time and detach from our electronics and just talk and listen to each other. We need to ask our children questions that will encourage them to talk to us. We need to ask open ended questions that will help us to learn more about the person that they are becoming. Questions such as:

- What makes them happy?
- What makes them sad?
- What are they thankful for?
- What are their goals?
- Who are they hanging out with? (Friend group)

- What is their favorite hobby?
- Who is their best friend?

Listening to our children will make them feel like they matter and that what they are experiencing matters.

When you feel like you matter to someone, it builds your confidence because you know that someone is in your corner. Most of all, teaching our children to listen, while listening to them, helps them to become more confident communicators. We need to know how they are doing, what they are feeling and how they are being influenced. This information will help us to provide more strategic guidance and encouragement.

"Listen to the whispers and you won't have to hear the screams."

Cherokee Proverb

Strategy Seven

Quality Time: Spend Time With Your Children

SPEND TIME DOING THINGS WITH YOUR CHILDREN

AND NOT

ALWAYS FOR YOUR CHILDREN.

Things I wish someone had taught me

We should do more with our children and less for our children. In the process we are teaching them what we know.

We appreciate and remember what adults did **with** us more so than what they did for us.

Too often, we spend time doing things for our children because we love them, and we also want to get the job done quickly so that we can move on to something else. When we do things for our children, we are not teaching them how to do it, and most often, they will not gain a genuine appreciation for the work that we do for them. When we do things with our children, we help them build the skills that they need to become successful adults. I am talking about simple things like learning to sweep, cooking, changing a light bulb, organizing a closet or cabinet. All of these are tasks that you can spend quality time with your child. They may not like doing these tasks and they may not want to do them, who cares, make them do it any way. They will thank you for it later. Make them help you with the smallest tasks, like sweeping, to larger tasks like planning and preparing meals or yard work. It all counts as quality time.

"Tell me and I forget. Teach me and I remember. Involve me and I learn."

Benjamin Franklin

Strategy Eight

Hug Your Children

HUG YOUR CHILDREN

HUG THEM OFTEN

AND

CONSISTENTLY

I'M ALWAYS HERE

Hugging our children lets them know that we are there for them. We should hug our children often and consistently. There is actual research that reveals the benefits of hugging our children. Dr. Emily Mudd a Psychologist with the Cleveland Clinic Children's (2020), stated that "We know that even from the moment we're born, that touch, physical touch, attention, and hugs, are so very important for both nervous system regulation, and brain development." Dr. Mudd further stated that, research has shown that when we receive a hug, our brains release oxytocin – which is the 'feel good' brain chemical. A hug can also help children manage stress, by calming the release of cortisol – which is the stress hormone.

In my experience, one of the biggest confidence boosters, is to know that you have someone in your corner that is going to be there for you. One of the most assured ways that we show our loved ones that we are there for them, is by giving them a hug, especially when they are hurting, disappointed, or have experienced some type of trauma or lost. Hugging our children is one of the best investments that we can make to help them build emotional fortitude and confidence.

It is easier to get up and give it another try when you know that someone is cheering for you or knowing that you have the support that you need to regain your courage. Make sure that we make time to hug our children, including our boys. Boys need hugs too.

Strategy Nine

Teach Your Children What You Know

TEACH YOUR

CHILDREN

WHAT

YOU

KNOW

LISTEN
AND
LEARN

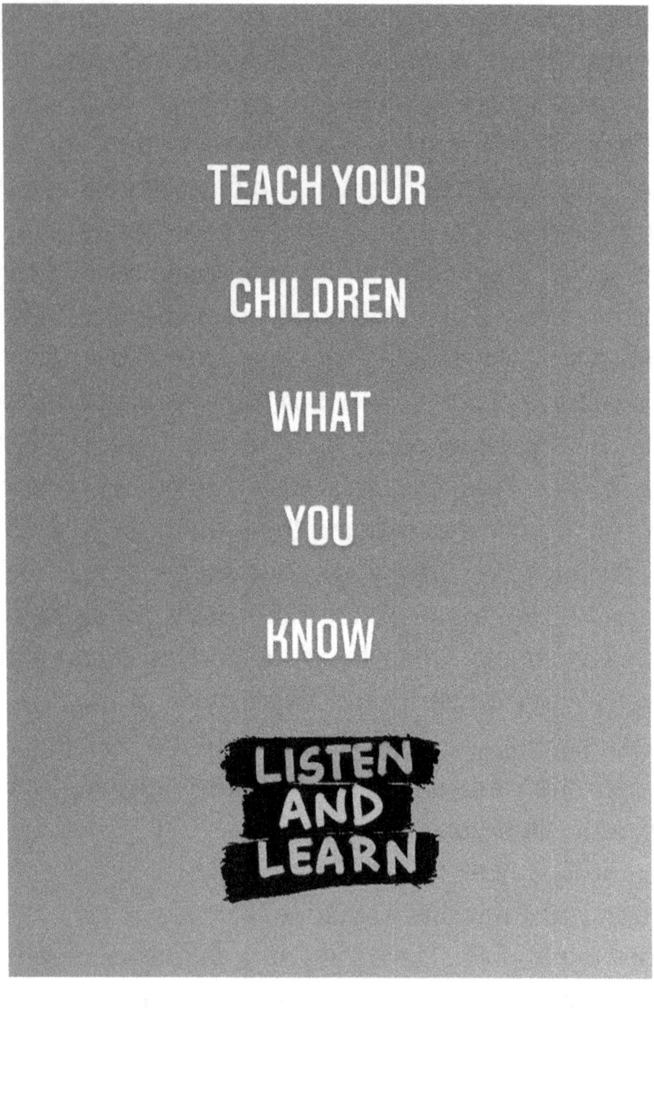

Teaching our children what we know is one way to make sure that they can take care of themselves when they are grown and out on their own. When toddlers gain their motor skills, they want to help do everything, and sometimes we allow them to help because it is cute and fun. Once they become children and adolescents, we tend to allow their schedules to determine how much we ask them to do. When we teach children what we know, it is one investment that we know will build their confidence because we know that they will be able to take care of themselves. We need to teach our children how to:

- Cook
- Clean
- Manage money
- Invest
- Save
- Spiritual self-care
- Buy groceries
- Look for bargains
- Read
- Work/Life Balance

These are just a few of the things that we should teach our children that will not be taught in school. If you do not know how to do some of the skills listed above, now is the time to learn. You all can even learn together. We are working hard to leave our children a legacy, and we need to raise them so that they will know what to do with it. Teach them!

Strategy Ten

Develop a Growth Mindset

Developing a growth mindset in our children is probably one of the most valuable investments that we can make in our children. Some people believe the growth mindset is about being positive, and yes, that is part of it. The growth mindset is more about effort and one's ability to see challenges as an opportunity to learn and grow, rather than seeing challenges as a threat. When we view challenges as a threat, we tend to stay away from them for fear of not looking smart or being seen as not capable. That is more aligned with a fixed mindset.

A person with a growth mindset sees challenges as an opportunity to learn and get better, faster and stronger at their craft or whatever they are trying to accomplish. Helping to develop a growth mindset in our children will allow them to experience life more abundantly. The growth mindset will give them the courage to try new things, not fear a challenge, and to not see competition as a threat. We want our children to embrace challenges and to learn from others that may have skills that they have not acquired yet.

We are back at the word "YET." The word yet, is particularly important when teaching our children to have a growth mindset. When we teach our children to say, "I have not learned this yet" instead of "I cannot do this," it leaves open the door for learning and growth. The fixed mindset shuts the door to possibilities and deepens doubt. Developing a growth mindset in our children takes time and effort. We must choose our language and our reactions to situations wisely. What we say and how we react to challenges, is what they will learn. Some examples of growth mindset language are:

- I will try again.
- What can I do better next time?
- Did I do my best?
- I tried really hard; I'll do better next time.
- I do not know how to do that yet?
- Mistakes help me learn.
- I can always improve.

The bottom line is, we need to let our children know that being proficient or excellent at something requires effort and not luck.

Carol Dweck (2006) states that the passion for stretching yourself and sticking to it, even when it is not going well, is the hallmark of the growth mindset. This is the mindset that allows people to thrive during some of the most challenging times in their lives.

Conclusion

Parents, teachers and mentors alike, are continually looking for ways to help our children become the best possible version of themselves. Throughout my career and as a parent, I have found that it is important that we engage our children and make sure that they are full participants in their development. When we do everything for our children or make excuses for our children, we hurt them instead of helping them. Children need to learn from their challenges to grow. No matter how difficult it is for children when they are challenged, we should encourage them to try other strategies and work harder rather than make excuses for them.

Nothing replaces hard work, character, integrity and the ability to work well with others. We all want our children to be resilient, confident and happy. We must develop our children to know that happiness is not always having fun and being carefree. Happiness is also the ability to accomplish goals and feel confident in our abilities to have a quality life. Happiness is a by-product of being confident, successful and secure.

It is my sincere hope that this book offers some strategies that will help all of us to become more confident parents, teachers, and mentors. When we develop our children's resilience and confidence, we also help to make a better world.

Sources

Cleveland Clinic, Newsroom (2020). How A Hug Can Help Your Child.

https://newsroom.clevelandclinic.org/2020/01/20/how-a-hug-can-help-your-child/

Dweck, Carol S. (2006). Mindset: The New Psychology of Success, How We Can Learn to Fulfull our Potential. Ballatine Books, New York.

Morgan Stanley, Wealth Management (2016). When Little Geniuses have Big Dreams.

https://www.morganstanley.com/articles/little-geniuses-big-dreams?&cid=ppc-71700000045240996:700000001822702:58700004654357395:p39240828650&msclkid=40a6b35d15061783ddd2ece05141e4d5&gclid=40a6b35d15061783ddd2ece05141e4d5&gclsrc=3p.ds

www.ingramcontent.com/pod-product-compliance
Lightning Source LLC
LaVergne TN
LVHW020313110826
845148LV00017BA/2657

* 9 7 8 1 7 3 6 7 9 8 9 0 4 *